SPARE ME!

PORTRAIT OF A BOWLING FANATIC

SPARE ME!

PORTRAIT OF A BOWLING FANATIC

DAWSON TAYLOR

ILLUSTRATIONS BY

GARY PATTERSON

A FULL CIRCLE BOOK

CONTEMPORARY
BOOKS, INC.
CHICAGO ▪ NEW YORK

The authors would like to thank Jim Ardito of The Right Writers, Inc., Chicago, for special contributions.

Published by Contemporary Books, Inc.
180 North Michigan Avenue, Chicago, Illinois 60601
Manufactured in the United States of America
International Standard Book Number: 0-8092-5017-9

Published simultaneously in Canada by Beaverbooks, Ltd.
195 Allstate Parkway, Valleywood Business Park
Markham, Ontario L3R 4T8 Canada

CONTENTS

1
THE SLANGUAGE OF BOWLING

Walk into a bowling alley on league night uninitiated, and you're likely to think you're traveling overseas. Not so much because someone's hanging over a railing getting sick, but because absolutely no one is speaking English. At least not the English *you* learned.

There is a distinct slanguage to bowling, a veritable babble-on of weird words and phrases that sound totally foreign to the novice bowler. Don't panic. You *can* speak native tongue. Just pick up the slang and heave it around like your bowling ball. To help you, here are some common phrases you might hear between the crashing of pins and leveling of the usual obscenities.

"OK, Mabel, slam that dinner bucket!"
Bowlers are innovative, but tossing a bucket of fried chicken at the pins hasn't yet become accepted technique. Actually, the "dinner bucket" isn't food at all—it's a leave of the 2-4-5-8 cluster which is makable.

P.S. Surely, you must be careful whom you're calling Mabel. Also be careful whom you're calling Shirley.

"You useless Chinaman! You've chopped off your mother-in-law!"

This sounds like dialogue right out of a Brian DePalma film. What's going on out there? you may wonder. Are Chinamen being chopped up in bowling alleys all over the United States? What have Chinamen got against their in-laws, anyway? Are they turning into outlaws, or what?

Of course not! No ethnic slurs are intended here at all. Bowling is America's melting pot. "Chinaman" is merely the quaint little tag given to the player who bowls in the number three position on a five-man team. The "mother-in-law" is the 8-pin in the back row. And to "chop off" a pin simply means to leave it standing. Obviously, then, no one should be offended by this remark. Not even by the fact that once a Chinaman chops off a pin, a half hour later it's standing again. Oops. . . .

THE MOTHER-IN-LAW

"We've still got a chance—she's hung out the clothesline."

Obviously, there's good news here. Hanging out the clothesline may mean it's laundry day and you can finally get the pizza stains off your bowling shirt. It could also be a subtle hint that you're suffering from ring around the collar, a fate worse than a string of gutter balls. However, if you choose "none of the above," you are correct. The "clothesline" is an orderly (but despicable) leave of the 1-3-6-10 or 1-2-4-7 pins. It's tough but distinctly makable. Just be careful not to leave the 1-2-10 group standing, or you will have what is known as a "washout." Make the "clothesline," and you could take your opponents to the cleaners. That should take the starch out of the stuffed shirts!

THE CLOTHESLINE

"Another hand of double pinochle, Sam?"
The sarcasm in the voice of the speaker leaves little doubt of his intention. Leaving the "double pinochle" means you've got the 4-6-7-10 split on your hands. If you leave it too often, your team members are likely to insist you take up croquet and leave the bowling to those who still have some of their marbles.

THE SPLIT

"Oh, no! He's going for Grandma's teeth!" Bowlers may be aggressive, but they hardly ever leap to another lane to rip out the dentures of a senior citizen taking too long to bowl. That would be uncalled for. No, "Grandma's teeth" is merely a leave of the ragged 4-6-7-9-10 cluster (also known as the "Polish cathedral" or the "Greek church"). To extract "Grandma's teeth," get a Polident grip on the ball, set your choppers, and let it fly. Bowlers should note that this can be an effective technique when used in a conscientious program combining bowling clinics and regular professional care.

GOING FOR THE KILL

"He's off to Kresge's again."
In bowling circles it's considered impolite to leave in the middle of a game to go discount shopping. You may want to do so after being called a "Kresge," however, since it is a tribute to your bowling skill—or, rather, lack thereof. The "Kresge" is the 5-10 split, which is at least better than a "Woolworth," the cheapest split in town.

"Nice foundation, Marge!"
Are Marge's undergarments clearly visible to the world? Is it time for Slenderalls, or what? Is Marge to be pitied or shunned? Not really. Actually, Marge is receiving a compliment here. A "foundation" in bowling is a strike in the ninth frame, which may lead to three more in the tenth and "topping out," as it were. Bottoms up, Marge!

2
A BOWLER'S PRAYER

Oh, Lord of the Lanes please hear me,
Before I start out to bowl,
If you drop that pin and spare me,
I'll gladly sell my soul.

A BOWLER'S PRAYER

3
FUN FACTS
ABOUT BOWLING

Today, nearly 12 million Americans bowl at least once a week.
A staggering statistic. It's verifiable, though, if you've ever tried to get a lane on league night. You need to sign up early. You've got 12 million Americans in the line ahead of you.

The average bowler is 33.3, makes $25,000 a year, is married 71 percent of the time, has 1.3 children, and owns his own home.
The most interesting statistic here is the fact that the average bowler is "married 71 percent of the time." Obviously, 29 percent of the time, married guys aren't owning up to it. It can also be concluded that bowling regularly leaves you little time to have a whole second child. Understandable. Bowling comes first.

A BAD NIGHT

U.S. PRESIDENTS AND BOWLING

George Washington—Reputed to have had wooden balls.

Abe Lincoln—Made the Gettysburg Address short because the Log Cabin Boys were bowling that night against Al's Emancipation and Lubrication Station.

John F. Kennedy—Most famous for the Cuban Bowling Crisis, during which the Soviets shipped in nuclear balls with true first strike capabilities.

Richard Nixon—Once bowled two perfect games in a row, though the record of this was erased.

Gerald Ford—Considered the most dangerous presidential bowler. To bowl with Ford was to take both the ball and your life in your hands.

Jimmy Carter—Once admitted to having his mind in the gutter ball.

Ronald Reagan—Starred early in his career in the famous movie *Bonzo Goes Bowling.*

4
THE TEN
COMMANDMENTS
OF BOWLING

1. Thou shalt not have false gods before thee. Carmen Salvino is it!
2. Thou shalt honor thy league night above all others.
3. Remember, it is easier for Satan to enter the Kingdom of Heaven than to make the 7-10 split.

4. Walk not beyond the foul line, for it is hallowed ground.
5. Honor thy sponsor and plug him.
6. Thou shalt not covet they neighbor's form, no matter how curvaceous.

7. Good sportsmanship is next to godliness and next to impossibleness also.
8. No matter how badly thou art losing, thou shalt not bounce a ball off thy competitor's head.
9. Drink is the devil's playground. Beware the teeter totter.
10. Thou shalt commit adult-ery at all times. Adult behavior in bowling is a rarity and devoutly cherished.

SPORTSMANSHIP

5
BOWLING
BADGES OF COURAGE

Badges? Bowlers don't need no stinking badges! It's enough to play the game. Ha, ha, ha, ha, ha. Who are we kidding? Bowling trophies and awards are as important as breathing to a bowler. Maybe more so. Threaten to take away an award, and he'll hold his breath till his face turns blue. Recognizing this, there are some special awards given by the American Bowling Congress. They're presented for high scores or accomplishing big feats. No award is given for fitting big feets in the shoe rental department, but those people are usually feted in other ways.

- For rolling a 300 game, 12 strikes in a row, the reward is a 10-carat gold ring with a tiny diamond in it. For rolling two perfect games in a row, the reward is immortality!
- For rolling a 299 or 298 score, a similar ring is awarded but with no diamond. A toupee is also presented if the bowler wrenched his hair out when the last two stupid pins wouldn't fall!
- For rolling a score of 700, a chevron and certificate of achievement are given. A Chevette used to be given, but the budget was cut.

- For converting the "Big Four" split, the 4-6-7-10, you get a chevron. For converting 10 heathen tennis players to bowling you receive a free game—no strings attached.
- For converting the 7-10 split, you get another chevron and the famous "Attaboy" pat on the back, which is worthless.
- For rolling 11 strikes in a row, the award is a black leather belt and belt buckle. Black leather pants and whip follow.

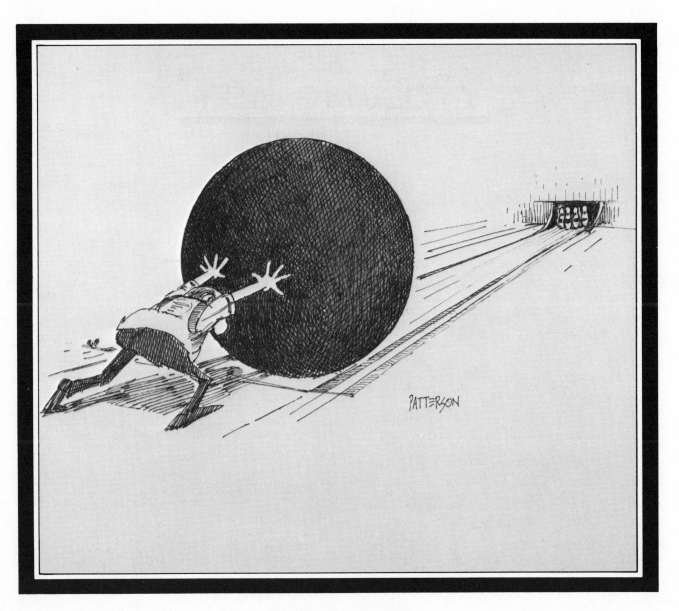

DETERMINATION

6
A ROGUE'S GALLERY

THE CRANKER

Want to get cranky in a hurry? Bowl with The Cranker. The Cranker is big. He's a Paul Bunyan kind of guy. Unfortunately, he has the brains of Babe, The Ox. Kind of smells like Babe, too, but you can be the one to tell him.

Recognizable Cranker characteristics include a size 50 chest crammed into a size 36 shirt. He has fat fingers, fat wrists, and a fat head. But mostly, The Cranker is known for his power.

As he lines up, he licks his lips in anticipation of his upcoming display of raw power. Beginning his approach from near the men's room, he moves rapidly to the foul line, taking 30 to 40 tiny steps, each one coming faster than the preceding one.

At mid-backswing, the ball is three feet above his head. It's brought down with such force and velocity that spectators are sucked in by the slipstream. The ball is thunderously released and propelled at least 15 to 30 feet in the air, where it finally crashes with enough of a jolt to knock all the pins down without touching them. It's a strike every time with The Cranker, and who's gonna call him on a technicality?

THE CRANKER

THE MECHANIC

The Mechanic has every tool and gadget available in the bowling game. This inventory is supplemented by his own ingenious creations, whipped up in his basement bowling laboratory. The scenario for these inventions is typical. The wind howls. Thunder cracks. The room buzzes with electronic gizmos. Igor laughs hysterically as The Mechanic madly inserts the brains of a computer into a bowling ball. Surely, this will mean the ultimate in precision. A 300 game every time. But something goes wrong. The ball runs amok. The Mechanic is declared completely insane by the townspeople and therefore qualifies for president of the local bowlers' club.

TAKING AIM

As further proof of insanity, here's a compendium of items that The Mechanic must have on hand at all times, whether he's bowling or not:

- a small can of Johnson's Baby Powder for sticky approaches
- a rosin bag for his grip
- a small jar of rosin mixed with wax for an even greater grip
- a wrist harness made of steel and vinyl
- various inserts of plastic and/or rubber for altering the size of finger holes
- a rattail file for enlarging finger holes
- fine sandpaper for smoothing finger holes
- fingers for putting into finger holes
- space-silicone soles to prevent sliding feet
- a small bag of calcium silicate to absorb moisture in his bowling bag
- a huge bag of calcium silicate to absorb moisture from the atmosphere
- a bowling glove with a padded palm
- a separate carrying case for credit cards, since cost for these and other items runs around $100 billion a year

CANNONBALL EXPRESS

THE BALLET DANCER

A closet ballet star, this bowler is the joy of culture lovers and fanny fanciers. The female of the species is typically spotted wearing jiggle-hugging warm-up pants or crowd-stopping Hawaiian clam-diggers. The male of the species is less colorful but equally entertaining.

Performing to some internal music—the likes of which is most likely weird—The Ballet Dancer looks like she's ready for a *pas de deux* (father of two) as she readies herself for the approach. She raises the ball to the fifth position, pirouettes three times on her way to the foul line, then dumps the ball with a graceful thud. Unfortunately, she will not bowl again unless summoned by cries of "Encore," making her a prima bowlerina in anybody's book.

FINESSE

THE DUMPER

The Dumper is usually a big galoot, clumsy and lumbering and more than six feet tall, unless he's shorter. The Dumper's name is derived from the fact that he never rolls the ball; he launches it! Consequently, the ball lands with the force of a mini-megaton, creating rather large craters in the lane. For this reason, The Dumper is hardly the alley owner's favorite person. Watching your bowling alley being destroyed by a dumping maniac is hardly a fun way to pass the evening. "Hey, you!" the owner shouts, "learn to release the ball properly, will ya?! Why don'tcha bowl somewhere else!" To which The Dumber responds, "Sure!"—then dumps the ball on the owner's foot!

THE DUMP

THE HUSTLER

"Gosh, did you see those pins all go down? How did that happen? And with all that money on the line, too. What a lucky break!"

Sure, and if you really believe it was lucky, we've got a bridge we'd like you to see. Sweet, innocent, wide-eyed exclamations like these can mean only one thing: you're dealing with the bowling Hustler. BEWARE! Hang on to your wallet, your underwear, your girlfriend, and your false teeth. Nothing's safe or sacred around The Hustler. Watch for these warning signs:

- a velvet-lined bowling bag
- bulging eyes and a bulging wallet
- overuse of "Golly!"
- severe salivation around bowlers with low averages
- a little black book filled with computer print-outs of past performances.
- the immortal words, "Hey, why don't we up the stakes?"

Any of these indicate The Hustler's on hand, with his hand soon to be in your pocket.

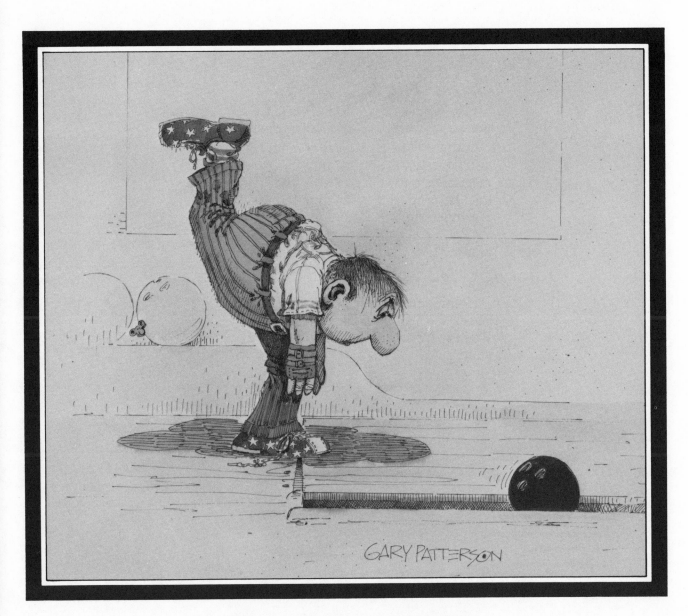

THE HUSTLER (AT PRACTICE)

Count on The Hustler to come through with a strike when the chips, your car, your mortgage, and your first-born child are on the line. Be prepared as the impossible 7-10 split is somehow made. Count on the Red Sea and the 2-4-5-8 cluster to be parted. And rest assured that the last part of the game that's *already been decided* will witness a few gutter balls by The Hustler.

Helping to recognize The Hustler helps. Check the "Wanted: Dead or Mortally Wounded" posters that hang in every bowling alley.

THE HUSTLER (IN COMPETITION)

THE TIMID SOUL

Intimidated by impossible splits? By the ability and confidence of "regular" bowlers? By the "in" crowd on league nights? By the prospect that you'll never be one of the guys, even if you are a woman?

Take heart in the amazing tale of Bertha Mae Hickenlooper. Bertha Mae was an unmarried schoolmarm who had never engaged in sports of any kind. Although she was pushing her prime, she still had hopes of catching some eligible male and decided to try bowling as the means to do it.

She arrived at Ebb and Flo's Bowling Emporium in Flint, Michigan, on a fateful night in December, 1986. Bertha not being exactly a "looker," few men in the alley looked her way as she took to a lane and let her first ball fly. The results were hardly momentous. Her ball proceeded fairly well down the middle of the lane and entered the 1-3 pocket. A moment later, all the pins fell except the 5, 7, and 10—leaving, as all serious bowlers know, a truly impossible split. If the 5-7 split is converted, the 10-pin stands. If the 5-10 split is converted, the 7-pin stands. In either case, bowlers are left holding an open frame.

In the annals of bowling, this split has never been converted by bowling man, woman, or beast, but that did not deter Bertha Mae. A few of the local boys noted her predicament and chuckled smugly.

This made Bertha Mae all the more determined. She gritted her teeth, stepped up, and let her next ball go. What happened then was no less than miraculous.

Her ball struck the 5-pin on its right side. The 5-pin was deflected into the 7-pin, which struck the left sideboard and began, yes, began to roll across the lane toward the 10-pin. The guys stopped chuckling. They held their

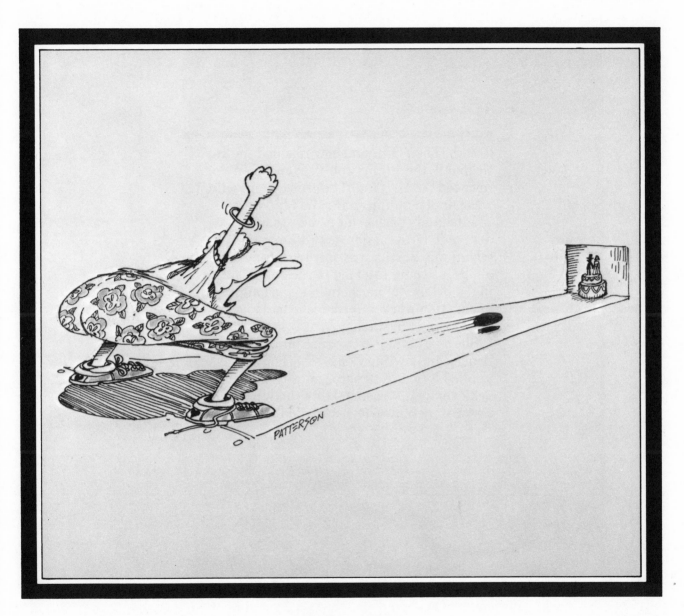

TIMID SOUL

breath. The 7-pin somehow reached the 10; it tickled it; the 10-pin wobbled; and then—oh, my goodness!—it fell! The crowd went wild. It was pandemonium as Bertha Mae was immediately besieged by 50 guys who demanded instruction on this amazing technique. Bertha was only too happy to oblige, offering tutoring to each of the 50 guys in the privacy of her home. It was tough, exhausting work, but someone had to do it, and Bertha Mae managed as best she could.

She also managed to cause quite a stir at the American Bowling Congress when she applied for a 5-7-10 patch signifying her great achievement. It seems that although other arm patches have been awarded for spectacular bowling accomplishments, like the "Big Four" conversion of the 4-6-7-10 and the "Triplicate Award" for rolling three identical games in a row, no patch existed for the 5-7-10 combination. Bertha Mae insisted they recognize her feat. They refused. She sued, and in a landmark decision the American Bowling Congress was finally forced to issue what is now known worldwide as the Hickenlooper decal.

All in all, it was an amazing lesson in nonintimidation, from which even the most timid souls can take heart. There's even a double-happy ending. Bertha Mae *was* eventually married. She is also the only bride ever known to have worn a bowling patch on the sleeve of her wedding gown.

7
HOW TO CHOOSE A WINNING BOWLING TEAM

1. Make sure you're named team captain. That way you can do whatever you want.
2. Get a list of the serious bowlers in town. If the list is blank, you're in serious trouble.
3. The first slot you should fill is that of anchorman. Here you're not looking for someone who can do the six o'clock news. You're looking for someone who won't choke, someone who will come through for you in the 10th frame when you need that big strike to win. Unfortunately, such an individual is rather difficult to find. If you can't uncover someone who always comes through, find someone who always buys the drinks. That way you can drown your sorrows when the anchorman does choke!

5-MAN TEAM

4. Next, you're looking for a sparkplug to put in the lead-off position. This is someone who will rev up the team with a mark right away. Watch out for the sputterer, the misfirer, or anyone who fuels up with a gallon of ethyl alcohol before frame one. These types can blow up in your face—especially the last guy, who can blow up the whole town!

5. Now you simply need two more players to complete the team. This is the center of your lineup, so you want dependability there. Solid bowlers. Steady bowlers. Not necessarily the hero type, but real workhorse kind of guys. The kind of guys who are chomping at the bit to come through, who are feeling their oats, who love to plow those pins down. They can be found. Check race tracks; sign up anybody whose name is Dobbin and anyone who picks up his ears when being called a horse's ass.

6. There are some general rules of thumb to follow when selecting players for your team.
   - Never pick anyone with a big, fat thumb.
   - Never sign up anyone whose nickname is "Bruiser."
   - Never pick a guy who talks a big stick, but when put to the test, melts under the pressure.
   - Never ignore your "gut" instincts about the potentiality of a bowler. If you *feel* he belongs on your team, go with it. We're reminded of a bowling captain who felt that way about a player who just happened to be blind. He went with him anyway, and in the finals of a big tournament, you know what heppened? The blind guy gutter-balled out! What else can you expect?
   - Never forget that bowling is just a game. Ultimately, selecting a winning team isn't as important as just getting out there and sharing this great sport together. Camaraderie and good, clean fun is what it's all about, isn't it? Right, and bowling a 300 is easy.

PRESSURE

8
THROWING
THE BIG CURVOLA

1. Practice a roundhouse arm action, instead of the straight-line arm action of normal bowlers. Besides giving you the right spin, this has the advantage of making sure you're not crowded while you bowl.
2. Buy some of those nifty bowling gloves that the pros wear. They won't help you bowl better, but they will prevent the entire surface layer of your hand from being ripped off as you release the ball.
3. Use the heaviest ball available and throw it as hard as you can. The Big Curvola is hard to aim, so take advantage of the seismic tremors created from its impact with the back wall—good for at least eight pins.

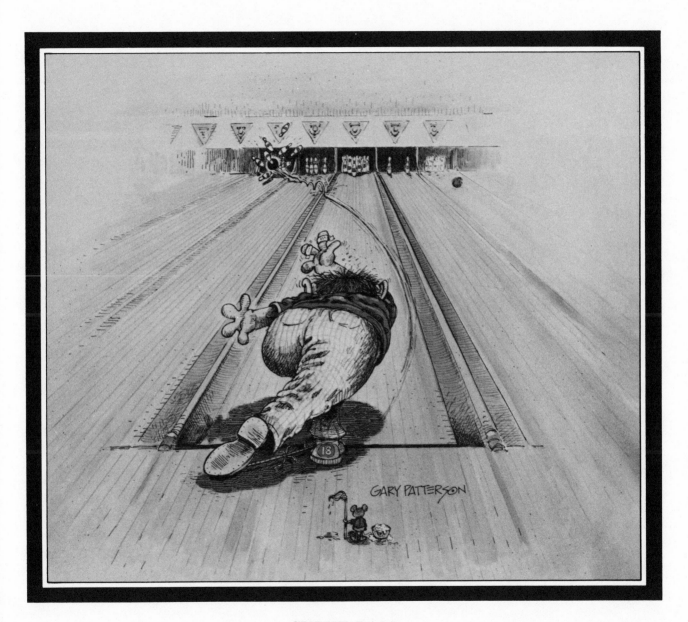

CURVE BALL

THE MARK OF A GOOD BIG CURVOLA

Bowling scientists have spent years charting the path of the perfect Big Curvola:

Stage 1: Launch

The 54-pound ball leaves the bowler's hand at a precise 45-degree angle and tears off at high speed across three lanes. The Big Curvola bowler is well aware that this plays hell with his neighboring bowlers' concentration.

Stage 2: Course Trajectory Change

Spinning at approximately 2,000 revolutions per second, The Big Curvola stops dead in the third lane, smoke pouring from its finger holes.

Stage 3: Second-Stage Burn

Accelerating at 500 miles per second per second, the ball nears the speed of sound as it approaches the pins.

Stage 4: Impact

The ball breaks the speed of sound and is traveling at Mach 6. The sonic boom knocks down people's drinks, ladies' girdles, a side wall—everything but the pins. Crashing into the back wall, the impact starts a nuclear chain reaction, melting every pin—a clean strike.

9
THE PRO SHOP

The first thing to remember about bowling pro shops is that they are run by people who spend their lives drilling little holes in hard round objects, into which people stick their fingers. This, along with selling bowling gloves, shoes, trophies, and balls, requires an IQ less than Einsteinian.

Something that few people are aware of, however, is the Bowling Shop Proprietors' Creed (as opposed to the proprietors' greed, which is another story). Every pro shop owner religiously follows these highly secret rules, and the penalty for divulging them is terrible indeed: proprietors must bowl an entire game with a ball they've drilled! Needless to say, not a single pro shop proprietor has ever spilled the beans.

Read the creed carefully. You will be tested.

THE PRO SHOP

NO BATHING

Soap and water are definitely taboo for pro shop orporietors.

Advantage: People never question bills or service or argue about finger holes drilled three sizes to small. The average time of interaction with nonbathing proprietors is 2.5 seconds. Shorter, if at all possible.

WEAR THICK GLASSES

Even those with 20/20 vision have to wear glasses with Coke-bottle lenses.

Advantage: This ensures that they never violate another part of the creed: always drill finger holes three sizes too small (see "No Bathing," above).

Additional Advantage: They can't see themselves in the mirror.

BAD BREATH

Any kind of oral hygiene is also taboo.

Advantage: Extremely useful in polishing hard-to-shine ball surfaces, as one blast can strip away material faster than sulfuric acid.

KEEP NOTHING USEFUL IN STOCK

This is perhaps the strictest segment of the creed. A typical shop has millions of items, from three-pronged pin diddlers to Albanian finger-hole glue. None of it looks good, makes sense, or proves useful.

Advantage: This makes a pro shop the perfect place for all your Christmas shopping.

10
MORE ROGUES

THE LOVER

Casanova, Don Juan, Richard Burton—
they've got nothing on Arnold "Stud"
Lipschitz, the hottest item to hit the lanes
since automatic ball return.

Arnold is a wonder to behold. Strolling in
late for maximum effect, he knows every
woman in the place is transfixed by his jet-
black curls (Grecian Formula and a home
perm); his Aztec sun-god tan ($200 a week for
a tanning booth); his hard, flat stomach (Mr.
Courtney's Girdles for Men); and his obvious
manhood (Sal's Meats—Kielbasa Our
Specialty).

Having received his training at the finest bowling studios in Europe, Arnold is poetry in motion: the practiced flick of the wrist to remove a piece of lint from his Saks bowling trousers; the delicate knee bend to retrieve the ball, maximizing visiblity of the derriere; and the elegant flourish of the handkerchief, gently polishing the ball to a beautiful shine— all designed to make even the most hardened bowling female swoon with lust.

Alas, Arnold bowls a 72 average and never scores. Every female in the place knows that he's married to Ethel "Cuddles" McGee, construction foreman and local arm-wrestling champion. The girls like Arnold, but they like life, too.

THE SNARLING TIGER

The Snarling Tiger is the unholy terror of the lanes. His poor sportsmanship and violent temper have caused him to be barred from dozens of bowling teams—including the Hell's Angels. Resembling more than anything else an oversized gorilla (except that gorillas aren't quite as hairy), The Snarling Tiger is the first to drink and the last to pay. Wearing metal-spiked, leather bowling shirts with slogans that say "Eat at Joes—or I Kill Ya," this paragon of virtue sets an example for all of us not to follow.

In wartime, The Snarling Tiger is the guy who gets medals for killing three to four hundred of the enemy with his bare hands. In peacetime, he gets 10-to-life for replacing a fellow bowler's head with his ball because the poor sot glanced at the Tiger's wife for more than three nanoseconds.

The Snarling Tiger does have some redeeming qualities, however. For a small fee he'll break the legs of the auto mechanic who charged you $452.73 for a used carburetor, and for only slightly more he won't break *your* legs for breathing too loudly while he's bowling.

11
HOW TO IMPROVE YOUR GAME

1. Buy every self-help bowling book you can lay your hands on. They won't help a bit, but you'll (1) know how truly worthless your technique is and (2) have something to burn in the fireplace this winter.

THE ALL-STAR

2. If you can't get better, get worse. Bowl as if you had the coordination of Gerald Ford (if you're reading this section, you probably do already) and obtain a huge handicap. This will infuriate bowlers who practice their technique 16 hours a day, especially when your 29 beats their 273. Don't however, do this when bowling against The Snarling Tiger (see preceding chapter) unless you really *want* to put your dentist in a higher tax brakcet.

RUSHING THE FOUL LINE

3. Buy every bowling accessory known to man: the Moroccan goat's-hair gloves, the French Kiss bowling bag, and the Libyan missile ball with pin-seeking capabilities. You'll still bowl like a nerd, but you'll be doing your part to promote international relations.

WHATEVER IT TAKES

BOWLER'S NIGHTMARE